Reflections on Life, Marriage, and Anger

Reflections on Life, Marriage, and Anger

Lester J. Bolanovich, M.D.

Reflections on Life, Marriage, and Anger

ISBN-13: 978-0-578-67875-7

Library of Congress Control Number: 2020907623

CIP information available upon request

First Edition, 2020

Managing Editor: Katie Elzer-Peters

Development Editor: Addy McCulloch

Proofreader: Stephen Wilson

Layout: Holly Rosborough

Cover Design and Artwork: Caroline Washburn

10 9 8 7 6 5 4 3 2 1

Dedicated to

Joyce Wilson Bolanovich

There is no grail more elusive or precious
in the life of the mind than the key to
understanding the human condition.

– E. O. Wilson, *The Social Conquest of Earth*

Contents

Preface

This book is a series of reflections on my experiences trying to help patients with their problems. It certainly does not pretend to be a scholarly work or a textbook. However, it is written with the intention of sharing with the reader some of the difficulties people encounter as they struggle with life's problems. The patient examples provided are limited to patients who are very much in contact with reality. I have avoided examples of severely ill people who are unable to maintain a sense of reality and consequently have difficulty engaging in the therapeutic process. However, similar dynamics can occur with patients who struggle with reality.

In accordance with HIPAA and privacy regulations as well as my own professional ethics, I have gone to great lengths to leave out material that would possibly identify my patients. The examples given will attempt to show what I believe to be a certain consistency in the way people choose their marital partners. Even with multiple marriages, there is a tendency to repeat the same mistakes encountered in the first marriage. Not only is it apparent in the selection of the marital partner, but it can also be seen in the dating history. I will explain this later in some of the clinical examples.

This book was written to illustrate some of the difficulties people have in relating to others in a harmonious way. Some points I make may very well have been said by others. I have tried to give credit to others when I was aware of that. However, if it has been said before by someone else then I am happy to apologize and confirm the same understanding.

In this book, I frequently discuss attachment to objects, human or otherwise. I am not able to summarize for the reader all the work that has been done in those fields of research. My descriptions of what may be similar may be simpler and are described in that tone.

If the reader would like to obtain a greater understanding about the subject, I recommend the second edition of the *Textbook of Psychoanalysis* (2012), Chapter 12 on object relations as summarized by Paul Williams, Ph.D.

The reader should recognize that when compared with the extensive and impressive research of talented psychoanalysts, I am attempting to explain complicated issues in a more straightforward way, using clinical examples in the hope of benefiting colleagues and others in the field. Only time will tell if these more simplified explanations have merit.

If the book does anything, I hope it will help people understand how much we need each other and how difficult it can be to bond with each other. It is much easier to be angry and pay the consequences because we are all afraid of being alone, and anger keeps us from dealing with the fear of being alone. Only bonding is the true healer. ▩

Acknowledgments

I would like to thank Andrew (Drew) Wilson, who provided preliminary editing and guidance through the early to middle stages of organizing the manuscript. He offered his expertise on phrasing and word choices, and he provided a good sounding board for the times when questions arose.

I would also like to thank my daughter, Susan B. Washburn, for typing the manuscript from my handwritten copy, updating and revising the manuscript as changes were made, and providing input and feedback on content. She was additionally instrumental in initiating and facilitating the publishing process with The Garden of Words.

A special thank you to my granddaughter, Caroline E. Washburn, for her original artistic interpretation of my idea for the cover.

Introduction

Perhaps most, if not all, of us have wondered about the reasons we behave as we do. My interest in our behaviors increased in college when I first began to read some of Sigmund Freud's writings about the effect of the unconscious mind on our behaviors. Although I have an abiding and deep respect for my psychoanalytic training, I have in many ways been eclectic in my approach to treating patients. While I may place different emphasis on certain analytic findings in this book, I remain a firm believer in the power of the unconscious mind to affect our behavior.

Over time in the course of my professional practice, I began to notice opposite characteristics among couples. For example, one spouse is always cold and wants the heat turned up, and the other is too warm and wants the window open. One spouse is better able to tolerate alcohol or anesthesia than the other. One spouse is more accurate in remembering the details of past arguments than the other. One spouse is more future oriented and the other is more focused on the immediate. One spouse is more of a disciplinarian than the other. In marriage, these differences may be bridged if the two partners are reasonable and motivated to accommodate each other; otherwise they become the marital playground where other, more significant differences are played out.

These differences are, in my opinion, genetically programmed and present at birth. In 2008, Steven A. Brown and colleagues reported at the National Academy of Sciences that differences between people who are "larks" (early risers) and "owls" (classic night people) can be detected at the molecular level from skin biopsy samples (Brown,

Kunz, Dumas et al., 2008). I reference this article to support my emphasis on the role of genes in the behavior of people.

My particular interest in these differences and the reason for attempting to write this small book has to do with the repeated observations that there is often a consistent pattern of people choosing a mate in marriage based on certain criteria. I maintain that caretakers marry caretakees. The caretaker is generally more empathetic, and the caretakee (my word) is less so. This observation is not limited to my patients. It can be seen easily in friends, relatives, acquaintances, and even strangers that you might meet in a chance encounter. I believe this particular difference in marriage partners is not sufficiently explored in psychiatric therapy. In this book, I describe the personalities of the caretaker and the caretakee and how they conflict with each other.

My observations overwhelmingly have been of heterosexual marriage partners. My limited experience working with homosexual partners has led me to the same observation. In other words, this dynamic is present in homosexual relationships, but I have no way of knowing if it is prevalent. Also, I want to make clear that I use the pronouns *he* and *she* in a general way, and not to assign or identify the sex of a caretaker or caretakee.

Later in the book, I give a description of personality characteristics more often, but not entirely, found in the caretaker, as well as characteristics of the caretakee. I attempt to show the various combinations that can come into play and how important it is for marital partners to be aware of and honest about their emotional needs.

The subject of marriage has been studied and written about for years by excellent researchers. What I am offering is simply my clinical impression. While I present clinical observations with some opinions I have regarding their nature, operation, and meaning, my observations do not necessarily offer pat solutions to the problems illustrated. My trepidation in attempting this book is tempered by the encouragement of patients, relatives, and friends who assure me it will be worthwhile. Analytic colleagues may criticize me for not being analytic enough. But then analysts have argued sometimes vehemently in their disagreements about analytic theory and practice. It has been said that

Sigmund Freud had to stop discussions about papers presented at meetings because the discussions could become too contentious and unfruitful.

Once again, my purpose is to describe some aspects of marriage that could be helpful to the lay public as well as mental health professionals. The institution of marriage has continued for many reasons, not the least of which is to protect, nurture, and educate children in preparation for adulthood and the survival of our species. I also explore what I think could be valid comparisons between the conflicts seen in marriage and the problems in other organizations. In order to protect the privacy of others I have disguised the identities of patients, friends, relatives, and their families. ▨

PART 1

Reflections and Explorations

Chapter 1

Caretaker and Caretakee

In the introduction, I described opposing behaviors among couples that can create stress or conflict if the couple is unable to reach a compromise. In situations such as these, I believe some people can make others symptomatic, i.e., depressed, anxious, or psychosomatic. It is not uncommon for the conflict to center around the personalities of caretaker and caretakee.

I would like to describe the characteristics of the caretaker personality and the caretakee personality and how they usually behave. This is not to say that there are no variations in the behavior of each, but for the most part they have rather distinct characteristics that define them fairly well.

I would like to define some of the terms I will be using. The word empathy is defined in the Webster's *New World College Dictionary* (2001, p. 466) as "the projection of one's own personality into the personality of another in order to understand the person better; ability to share in another's emotions, thoughts or feelings." When I am describing someone as a caretaker, I am describing a person who has more empathy than not. It is someone who thinks about the needs of others, primarily emotional but also physical needs. When I use the word caretakee (which I made up), I am defining a person who is less likely to be as empathetic and less likely to be oriented toward the needs of others. However, there are fluctuations and variations of the just defined personalities. The caretakers and caretakees as I have described them are born that way. With enough history of a family tree, it becomes easy to identify the respective characteristics in family members from generation to generation.

These characteristic personalities battle in families, marriages, friendships, schools, and workplaces. To repeat, empathy is the most defining characteristic. The caretaker is much more likely than the caretakee to possess that quality, and we can see how it manifests itself in the behavior of both.

The caretaker is more likely to clean up after herself. The caretakee is more likely to leave empty food dishes, coffee cups, etc., lying around rather than clean them or put them away. If the caretaker gets annoyed and complains about the caretakee's behavior, the caretakee will likely respond with, "Why does it bother you? I was going to do it eventually." Usually this conflict drags on. It is a contest. In essence, the caretakee is saying through her behavior, "You take care of me." The caretakee senses that the caretaker is eager to take care of others, so the caretakee tries to set the stage for receiving care, which can be a substitute for being loved.

The caretaker is much quicker to be aware of someone's needs, even if inconvenienced. The caretakee is less likely to go out of her comfort zone to help others. The caretaker is more apt to feel guilty if she can't take care of another. The caretakee views the caretaker as someone who can provide for the caretakee with little effort. The caretakee may be aware of others' needs, but likely is hesitant to help without limitations. The caretaker is more likely to be the disciplinarian in the family. The caretakee is less likely to use discipline, as he believes the children will love him more if he doesn't discipline them. The caretaker is more likely to be the record keeper and be responsible for the family finances.

The differences in what each brings to the relationship eventually become a source of conflict. For example, the caretakee begins looking to spot some flaw in the caretaker to balance the larger flaws in himself.

In a conversation, the caretakee often neglects to be specific in identifying the person he is describing. He often uses the pronoun he, she, or they as though the caretaker knows or can read his mind. When the caretaker asks for more specific details, the caretakee responds, "You are just not listening." This is the caretakee's way of setting a trap to anger the caretaker.

In general, the caretakee is a master of passive-aggressive behavior, whereas the caretaker is usually more direct and less passive-aggressive in dealing with others. When a caretaker comes for therapy, she is wary of me and what our relationship will be. It is most likely that she is not aware if she is a caretaker or caretakee and, likewise, she is not aware of whether or not I am a caretakee or caretaker. As we work together in psychotherapy, her anxiety subsides. She becomes aware of how she operates and identifies herself usually as a caretaker.

Caretakers are more likely to come to therapy because they are being drained emotionally by the caretakee. The caretakee doesn't like to admit this neediness and will seek help by passive-aggressively finding ways to drain the caretaker. She will say she doesn't need to see the psychiatrist because she isn't "crazy." In general, the caretakee is always looking to point out to the caretaker how he is inadequate. This is designed to shake the confidence of the caretaker. The biggest fear the caretakee has is the loss of the caretaker. So the excessive and often ill-founded criticism is meant to shake the confidence of the caretaker and keep him from leaving the excessive neediness of the caretakee, perhaps for a more reasonable caretakee. The strategy often works until the caretaker (with the help of a therapist) catches on to the passive-aggressive behavior of the caretakee and makes a move to stop it.

The caretakee's passive-aggressive tactics can take many forms. If the caretaker complains that the caretakee is doing something upsetting to the caretaker, the caretakee often responds with, "I'm not like that but you are like that." The caretakee expects the caretaker to make important phone calls, fill out forms, and perform many, if not all, of the administrative tasks needed for household operations. The caretakee depends on the caretaker to be his calendar. "What is the date next Monday? What is today's date? When are we going out to dinner with Mary and John? When is my auto inspection due? When is my dental appointment?"

This list of characteristics of the caretakee is not complete, but it does demonstrate the ongoing need of the caretakee to use any excuse to get others to do things for him. Unfortunately, it is an unconscious admission of the caretakee that he can't get the love he wants in a bonding relationship so he will get a love symbolically by having others do for him.

Recently, in my work with caretakers explaining the problems with their caretakee partners, something new has occurred to me. I admit it is not something I appreciated before, but I believe it is very important and I regret not being aware of it earlier. As I have previously expressed, I believe caretakers and caretakees are born that way. They are genetically primed to fit the role of caretaker or caretakee as they struggle with the consequences. I have begun now to see that caretakees are, in general, unable to communicate with others as well as caretakers. It is as though they are more socially anxious because of their lack of emotional communication. This is inborn. The caretakee is somewhat jealous and angry of the caretaker's power to provide empathy for others.

There are variations in the dyad. Sometimes an exhausted caretaker may need to switch into a caretakee role to relieve her emotional discomfort. Or she might befriend another caretaker to help her until she recovers from her stress. Sometimes the distinction between caretakee and caretaker is not clear.

The Caretakee Therapist

The following is a description of a caretaker who had been dominated by her father and become very angry about it. She came to see me on referral by another psychiatrist who was leaving practice. That psychiatrist had been prescribing medication, but a therapist in the practice attended to the therapy. I agreed to see the patient as a favor to the psychiatrist because I predominately do my own therapy and my own prescribing with the same patient. I would like to describe how our relationship progressed because it might be of some value to therapists.

From the beginning of therapy, the patient was generally angry and didn't hesitate to show her anger to me. I knew the anger was covering her lifelong struggle with insecurity. I saw her at approximately six- to eight-week intervals. In spite of the fact that I was not technically her therapist, I still asked a lot of questions and got to know a great deal about her life. Eventually, I came to understand how she operated psychologically. In one session, I told her I didn't think the medication she had been taking was effective enough and I suggested she consider a higher dose. In an angry reply, she stated no to my suggestion. However, after several more visits she spontaneously agreed to a trial of an increased dose. The trial was effective and she experienced some improvement, which pleased us both. I think the interaction between us overcame some of the angry distrust she had on her first visit.

Some months later, the patient suddenly asked if I would consider seeing her for the psychotherapy as well as prescribing medication. I replied that I would if she first discussed it with her current therapist. She did, and then she began seeing me for both therapy and medication management. Our relationship dampened the distrust but not the anger. It became apparent to me that she was a caretaker who was angry about how she had been used in her family of origin. However, she failed to recognize the cause of the emotional drain on her, that she was the most giving emotionally in that family. The most needy emotionally was her father. As the caretakee, he was in denial about his dependence on her and instead treated her with a barrage of criticism. Never once did he acknowledge her worth. By identifying (in the transference) me as a father figure, it is no wonder that she was both angry and distrustful of me.

However, to get back to therapy and therapists. With time, it became obvious to me that the therapist she had been seeing was also using her as a caretaker. It was a repetition of the ongoing history of her life. In therapy with me, she came to understand why she was so angry at her previous therapist and likely presented that same anger to me on her first visit. The insight was put to good use, and she is now handling herself with others in a more healthy way.

It is probably easier to be a therapist if you are a caretaker rather than a caretakee. Caretakers are, in my experience, usually not consciously aware of how valuable their empathy is and how much it is sought after by caretakees (who are usually unlikely to acknowledge that they receive emotionally).

However, it is very important for the caretaker psychiatrist not to encourage emotional dependence on himself. We know the caretaker psychiatrist is programmed genetically to help the caretakee patient, but the therapist should seek to move the patient to self-confidence, to no longer needing the services of the caretaker psychiatrist.

Chapter 2

Caretakees in Disguise

A woman came to see me because of marital stresses. She and her husband were educated in the same professional field. She had finished her master's degree and was working full time. He had finished the work for his master's degree, but he was stalling on taking the next steps to obtain the certification for which he was qualified. Although her husband was employed, he was not working in their professional field. She was born a caretaker and was still being used by her family of origin. He was more of a caretakee.

At our meeting, the wife complained of the emotional drain on her to prod him into doing what he needed to gain his qualification. She was becoming more angry and frustrated with her husband's stalling behavior. She felt guilty about being on him so much, even though she felt prodding him was necessary. She stated (in his defense) "He often does things for me, such as housework, cooking, cleaning, and running errands." I then asked her if he liked to do those things. She replied, "Oh yes, he really enjoys doing them." My answer was, "You are saying he does the things for you that he likes to do but neglects the things you really want him to do." The insight was helpful. This behavior is typical of a disguised caretakee. His need to be employed at jobs requiring less empathy and less sociability was likely the reason he was postponing completing his qualifications. She realized that his emotional dependency on her only added to the dependency on her from other family members. She also realized she had to take steps to relieve the pressure on herself. Her husband was disguising his true caretakee personality.

Another brief example concerned a patient whose anger at her mother was repressed. During the course of our working together, I pointed out that some of her mother's behaviors would lead me to believe that she (my patient) was not consciously aware of the anger she felt toward her mother, who was exploiting her emotionally. This patient immediately came to her mother's defense and countered with, "Oh no, you are very wrong. I know my mother loves me. She and I do so many things together." However, the patient had to admit that the activities were almost entirely what her mother wanted to do, not what she, my patient, wanted to do. It became clear that her mother was using her as a caretaker in many other ways and not offering any real emotional warmth in return; instead of empathy, her mother offered only exploitation. Because the patient so much needed her mother's love, she had repressed her anger at her mother. The mother, a caretakee, was very clever at disguising her exploitation of the caretaker daughter. The caretakee mother used my caretaker patient to accompany her to activities she wanted to do, but not to activities the daughter wanted to do. I suspect the caretakee mother was socially inept and therefore relied on her daughter to supply empathetic sociability and reassurance. These games between caretaker and caretakee often go on endlessly.

Many years ago, a widowed grandmother came to see me because she was distraught to the point of being depressed. She gave a history of stress in dealing with the wife of her older son. Before the marriage, her daughter-in-law couldn't have been any nicer to her. After the marriage and the birth of several grandchildren, however, the daughter-in-law refused to allow the grandchildren to visit my patient and refused my patient visitation in their home. My patient was puzzled by her son's lack of initiative to insist that his mother be allowed to visit their home or that he be allowed to bring the grandchildren to the grandmother's home. I explained to my patient that her son was a very emotionally needy person and probably had always been more emotionally dependent on her, growing up, than she realized. In my opinion, her son did not have the personality of being able to form relationships in which he would be required to give more of himself emotionally. With the birth of his children, he became more emotionally dependent on his wife, who was a controlling caretaker. The controlling caretaker (as I call her) also doesn't have enough empathy for a more mature relationship. She depends on controlling the behavior of the caretakee partner. Many years ago when I saw the grandmother, she apparently had no legal recourse to force a visit. Fortunately for my patient, her younger son was soon to be married and hopefully grandchildren would be available to her.

The controlling caretaker is not the true empathetic caretaker. In my opinion, she is motivated to deny visits to the grandmother because she knows the grandmother is a true empathetic caretaker and the grandchildren would become attached to her. The controlling caretaker's neediness cannot tolerate losing any love to anyone out-side of her control.

It is not unusual for the controlling caretaker to give away his or her hand. The controlling caretaker slowly, very slowly, makes excuses for not visiting friends of the partner and avoiding social events with the partner's friends. The controlling caretaker does not disallow her own parents and family members to interact with the grandchil-dren. It is not unusual for the empathetic caretaker (in this case, the grandmother) to be envied by caretakees, and a controlling caretaker is actually a caretakee in disguise. A controlling caretaker can be a woman or a man, but in each instance I believe the controlling care-taker to be a caretakee in disguise.

Excessive Neediness in Caretakees

As I have said previously, caretakers generally marry caretakees. There are, of course, many degrees of neediness among caretakees. I would like to describe several examples that I believe illustrate behaviors of caretakees with considerable emotional neediness.

A middle-aged man, divorced with children, came to see me because his behavior with his girlfriend was becoming a problem. He was unable to convince himself that she was faithful to him, and he was stalking her. He stopped this behavior when she threatened to report him to the police. During the rather brief period I saw him, he began dating other women. As time progressed, he began dating one woman more consistently. He then asked one day why he was not jealous of her. I asked him, "Are you in love with her?" He replied no. Delusional jealousy as it usually is described may become manifest when a commitment is made, i.e. when the person has fallen in love. What follows afterward is the inability to trust that love. It is a problem of trust after a commitment. It is possible that a pathologically jealous person is a considerably more needy caretakee.

In another example, a female patient, who suffered and repressed a painful rejection very early in life, was still very angry about it and sought guidance. As a married mother of several children, she was suffering from the constant stress of her husband's accusations of her infidelity. I couldn't be of any help because the stress of his accusations wasn't going to stop, and she couldn't see a way of leaving him. Some medication helped to alleviate her anxiety, but of course the stress continued. After several years, she returned to see me for another, unrelated problem. In our conversation I asked about her husband's complaints of her supposed infidelity. She stated it was no longer a problem and she didn't understand why he stopped accusing her, but she was pleased to be free of the accusations. I told her he had probably fallen in love with another woman. She accepted that and had some ideas about who it might be.

To summarize, a caretaker should be aware if she observes early in a relationship that her lover is too demanding about knowing where she is at all times and with whom she is relating to normally. She may think it is sweet and cute, but it can be a warning of more to come. It could be the forerunner of pathological jealousy. This pathological jealousy is more likely to manifest in men than in women, though not exclusively. It becomes an even more serious problem if the man has a history of violence. He may seriously injure or kill his lover, especially if she tries to leave him. When there is any hint of pathological jealousy surfacing early in the relationship, it might be better to exit the relationship earlier than later. I am not aware of any satisfactory resolution of this problem with any kind of psychotherapy. I think it is fair to say that with the accusation of infidelity, there is an accompanying effect of anger being verbalized. Possibly a very early rejection in life with the attendant anger creates a distrust that is then repressed by the anger and gets played out forever on another person, who is always a substitute for the original person who appeared to reject him. Once again, it is the anger that solidifies the distrust.

Chapter 3

Concerns of the Caretaker

As stated earlier, caretakers can be drained by the over-demanding neediness of a corresponding caretakee. A fair question might be: Why doesn't the caretaker separate from the stress of an overdemanding caretakee? The caretaker needs to have a caretakee. The relationship in which the caretaker takes care of a caretakee does something that makes the caretaker feel more positive about himself as a person. It builds in the caretaker a greater feeling of confidence and self-respect. The following case example demonstrates that.

Some years ago, a man was admitted to our hospital service with a history of depression and suicidal ideation. Fortunately, he stabilized and was discharged soon thereafter. At his request, I agreed to treat him as an outpatient. He was unhappily married and had two children with his wife. During the time I was treating him, he decided to divorce his wife and did so without malice. He had an excellent relationship with his children. He had lost a job sometime before his admission to the hospital, but then found other employment. His aged, widowed mother, who had been dependent on him, died. With the changes in his life (i.e. the divorce, loss of his mother, his children building more of a life on their own), he searched for someone else to care for. He applied to an agency to be a big brother to an eight-year-old boy in a very dysfunctional family. It was in keeping with his need to take care of others that he worked to be helpful to that youngster.

Several years later, he began experiencing anxiety. In therapy, he admitted to himself and me how much he had lost in the past month. He stated that a male friend, whom he had known for 40 years and had helped over the last 15 years, died the previous month. Another

33

male friend who couldn't read had been having difficulty finding and keeping a job. My patient, recognizing that his friend was very good mechanically, steered him into a good job where reading was less important and mechanical skills were favored. Unfortunately, this friend also died – another painful death for my patient. In addition to these losses, the young boy he had helped through the big brother program was now a young adult and sadly preferred the company of his dysfunctional family. It was a great disappointment to have failed with someone he tried so hard to help.

Here was my patient, a long-standing caretaker with not enough people to care for. Although after his divorce he enjoyed the company of other women, in retrospect I don't think he found one that would mesh with his caretaker personality. An increase in anxiety and depression led to several hospitalizations. After hospitalization, he continued in the hospital aftercare program. I eventually lost contact with him, but I remained concerned about him. After about a year or so, I contacted one of his children and inquired about his mental and physical health. His child stated he was doing quite well. I asked about the treatment he was having so I could consider the same treatment for my patients presently and in the future. I was told he was in a senior citizen residence and "He is taking care of everybody."

The lesson to be learned is to never overlook the need for a caretaker to have a caretakee. It is my opinion that my patient was born with the personality of a caretaker.

Children born with the caretaker personality will be recognized in the family and can potentially be used by caretakees, which include parents as well as siblings. If a caretaker child is not exploited but instead appreciated for her caretaker personality, it can lead to healing, self-esteem, confidence, and independence. It can also assist her in having better control over how much she gives of herself to others, instead of allowing herself to be exploited by them. She will, in essence, have a better introspective image of herself. Although I have no way of proving it, I have been concerned that a caretaker, exploited rather than being appreciated as a child, may not rise in life to the success her talent could provide. It would seem that the excessive neediness in the family and the emotional drain on her will chain her to the family. The guilt instigated by the family can be too strong to pull away from, and this may stunt her ability to use other talents and be more successful in life.

Chapter 4

Example of a Dual Role

Occasionally someone may be a caretaker in one relationship and caretakee in another relationship. The next brief vignette gave both my patient and me a good laugh.

Jake is sitting in the family TV room watching a football game. His wife, Sally, calls from the kitchen, "Jake, can I get you something?" He responds, "No, I'm fine." Ten minutes later Sally calls, "Jake, are you sure I can't get you something?" He responds, "No dear, I'm just fine." Another ten minutes later she brings him a beverage.

When he shared this with me, my patient couldn't stop laughing, and we both realized his wife just couldn't help herself. At our next session, she came with him as she occasionally did and was quite helpful by adding history. When I brought up this vignette, Sally readily admitted to her behavior and we all had a chuckle. Sometimes caretakers can't help themselves as they look for someone to take care of.

We can see from this example that the wife is the caretaker and the husband is the caretakee. Both of them agree in this regard. With the arrival of a granddaughter, however, the husband's role changed. With the granddaughter he was an exemplary grandfather. He was very giving to her and she saw him as her favorite. They couldn't have been more happy with each other. It is a beautiful example of how, in this instance, they shared a bonding relationship that gave each of them fulfillment emotionally. My patient, usually a caretakee with his wife, became the caretaker with his granddaughter. However, with his wife he was still the caretakee. Because of social inadequacies, my patient (as a caretakee) could relate to a child better because doing so requires less sophisticated social relating.

Another example: A middle-aged man suffered an extremely traumatic childhood. The oldest of several siblings, he started life being the caretaker for his chronically depressed mother and his younger siblings. In addition, he suffered emotional abuse from his substance-dependent and very angry father. These experiences set in motion a behavior pattern of mixed features. The patient was, by genetic make-up, a kind and gentle person, but at times he could slip into a caretakee role and act passive-aggressively to get his emotional needs met. Before going on a business trip, his wife gave him a list of things she would like him to do for her while she was gone. When she returned, he happily presented her a list of what he had done for her. Unfortunately, he had not done the things she specifically asked him to do and, of course, she became angry. A second instance of this dual role occurred when his wife once again went on a relatively short business trip out of town. When she returned, she specifically requested that she not be bothered by telephone calls or any other intrusion because she had a great deal of work to accomplish. She closed the door to the room in which she was urgently preparing her work for the next day. The husband went about his business cleaning the house. While cleaning, he discovered a small piece of candy his wife enjoyed. Instead of listening to what she said and not bothering her, he knocked on the door to present the candy token. She became very angry and she berated him for disturbing her. I tried to point out how his behavior was passive-aggressive in nature. What I mean is that he was acting in an angry mode by doing the opposite of what she requested. He consciously believed he was being helpful, but actually he was angry at her for being away on her business trip and was showing his anger by denying her what she requested. As I said previously, my patient was still capable of being a caretaker. He continues to be drained by his aged and extremely emotionally dependent mother. He and his wife are still struggling to develop a more mutually rewarding relationship.

As in the earlier case in which the caretakee husband became a healthy caretaker grandparent, another patient, along with his wife, developed a beautiful relationship with a preschool boy. The boy is a child of an unmarried mother who was very emotionally needy herself. The boy's father was unsupportive. The mother needed a babysitter, and my patient and his wife generously gave their time to his care. My patient in particular gave of himself unreservedly, and the young boy responded to the care. My patient was an outstanding caretaker to this young boy, and they bonded in a similar way as my other care-takee patient and his granddaughter. ▦

Chapter 5

Bonding

The term bonding is important to the discussion of relationships. Therefore, I want to describe what I mean when I use the word. In Webster's *New World College Dictionary*, 5th ed. (2014, p. 168), the word bond is defined as "a binding or uniting force; tie [the bonds of friendship]." I view bonding as an emotional tie between two people in which there is a strong, reciprocal concern about the emotional and physical concerns of each other.

There are many possible components to such a relationship. Foremost is an empathetic concern for the other person. There is honesty, trust, kindness, patience, forgiveness, and tolerance of other's shortcomings. I believe there also has to be a commitment to recognize anger in oneself and refrain from returning the anger when provoked. This is most difficult to do for many of us. Later I explain why it may be difficult.

Bonding produces, gradually in each member, a positive image of oneself consciously and unconsciously. Gradually this more favorable image of the self brings with it a greater confidence in one's abilities and the execution of those abilities. Most importantly, those positive images reduce fears of abandonment, which in turn helps reduce attachment to anger. I elaborate on this later in the discussion of our attachment to anger, which I believe is vigorously expressed at birth.

If I ask my adult patients (both female and male) if they could have the choice between all the sex they could possibly want or a true bonding relationship that provides trust, love, and respect, they always immediately choose a bonded relationship.

In our present society we are neglecting a search for bonding and its potential benefits and relying more on other attachments in our environment. Consequently, we are settling for less emotional stability and we are loosening our attachments to each other. This lessening of bonding in our society encourages more anger between us. It is easier than bonding, but it is less fulfilling. Most of my patients and friends concur that we are less attached to each other. To repeat, decreased attachment to bonding creates more anger and more and more disrespect for each other. This is not healthy for any of us, or for our society and country. It is important to remember the words of Robert Anson Heinlein (2016): "A dying culture invariably exhibits personal rudeness."

Bonding is not a new idea. Schweitzer & Joy (1947) described men in fifth century (B. C.) China who traveled the empire preaching love and peace. Schweitzer & Joy (p. 73) quoted the philosopher Chang Tso-lin, who described the efforts of these travelers to "unite men through an ardent love in universal brotherhood."

This encouragement to bonding comes from religion, philosophy, ethics and morality. In the past, guidelines have come to us from various religious faiths. Examples include:

"Hurt not others with that pain which hurts yourself."
From the *Udanverga*, 5:18, (Buddhism) 560 B. C.

"One should always treat others as they themselves wish to be treated."
From the *Hitopadeesa* (Hindu), 3200 B. C.

"Thou shalt love thy neighbor as thyself."
Leviticus 19:18 (Judaism, Christianity), 1300 B. C.

"Love for your brother what you love for yourself."
Hadith 13 (Islam).

Here, I approach bonding from a possible psychological position to underscore how difficult it is to promote bonding and the part that anger plays in that difficulty.

Bonding is closely related to attachment, the way we attach ourselves to so many things, animate and inanimate. Any attachment (animate or inanimate) carries with it the potential for loss of the attachment. The loss of any attachment can bring out anger. The greater the attachment, the greater the loss and the greater the anger, whether it is recognized consciously or unconsciously. In particular, anger that reaches the level of rage can be terribly destructive. Konrad Lorenz (1963, p. 211) reminds us of the inherent anger in any relationship:

> *Poet and psychoanalyst alike have long known how close love and hate are, and we know that in human beings also the object of love is nearly always, in an ambivalent way, an object of aggression too.*

Trust is a vital ingredient of a bonding relationship. If trust is broken in a bonding relationship, the anger may be intense and overwhelming, as illustrated in a line by William Congreve (1697) (modernized from the original): "Heaven has no rage like love to hatred turned, nor hell a fury like a woman scourned." I believe a bonding relationship encourages the development of emotional maturity, which in turn helps us deal with a universal fear of abandonment, i.e., being left with no attachments.

Healthy relationships that lead to bonding and trusting relationships to the benefit of both parties are always at risk. We should also be aware that we each carry a river of anger consciously and unconsciously that can easily be ignited. So it behooves us to recognize that anger can slip out easily, and it further benefits us to be prepared to forgive lest we obstruct a possible healthy, trusting, bonding relationship.

Chapter 6

Attachment

In this chapter I present my thoughts on attachments and objects of attachments. The terms *attachment* and *attachment theory* refer to a specific body of research that began with John Bowlby's seminal work following World War II (1969, 1980, and 1988).

For our purposes, we will consider attachment to be defined as a process by which we show interest in something or someone from which we expect to receive pleasure, or at least a sense of well-being. That investment of interest (in either animate or inanimate objects) is made possible by something called *psychic energy*. Freud called the concentration of psychic energy on some person, thing, idea, or aspect of the self, *cathexis* (Strachey & Freud, 1961).

I look at attachments in perhaps a much simpler way. I theorize that this ability of humans to attach themselves psychologically to other humans is present in our genetic make-up. At the time of birth there should be, barring complications in the intrauterine life, a strong attachment of child to mother and mother to child. Certainly, serious medical problems or genetic conditions, such as intellectual disability, could disturb that attachment.

Barring complications, the life in the womb is one of perfect existence in the sense that all of our needs are met, with no effort on our part. It is the closest thing to a heavenly experience that we will encounter in our lives, and it will motivate us to recapture that experience throughout the rest of our lives. At the time of birth, the intensity of that first attachment has to give way to the reality of the world. From this results *birth trauma*, hypothesized as an experience of overwhelming anxiety for the newborn, which the newborn then represses.

Theorists such as Otto Rank have proposed that subsequent developmental crises arise from this traumatic loss (Gabbard, Litowitz, & Williams, 2012, p. 569). Sigmund Freud wrote that birth is the first danger to life, as well as the prototype of all the later dangers we fear; and this experience has left its mark behind it through that expression of emotion which we call *anxiety* (Strachey & Freud, 1961).

In addition to the anxiety that accompanies birth, there is considerable anger at losing the intrauterine attachment. The newborn is angry about the detachment from mother, brought about by birth itself and the struggle to find other attachments to reduce the natural anxiety and fear of being alone. From day one, each of us embarks on a lifelong journey of seeking attachments that will reduce our anxiety of abandonment. Any attachment will be sought if it gives us some relief or distraction from the fear of abandonment. Of course, the first attachment is to our mother, followed by other family members available to and interested in us.

In addition to our attachments to other humans, we initially form an attachment to our own body parts. Sigmund Freud believed that in the oral phase of psychosexual development there is pleasure in sucking, which is an attempt at attachment. Freud believed that this attachment progresses in several distinct phases (Strachey & Freud, 1961). One would expect the child to move its attention from one organ of the body to the next organ of the body. However, because the transition is not always fully accomplished, some people may remain stuck with a lingering pleasure of staying in one phase too long. All of this is just to say that the ego is always looking for any attachment it can find to derive pleasure that will ease the fear of abandonment. Sometimes the attachment remains, to some degree, throughout life and is easily observed.

However, in the course of our lifetimes we do not limit ourselves to only human attachment. Other animate objects such as dogs, cats, and many other animals will be available as objects. Nor do we limit ourselves to animate objects. The world is full of potential objects. If we are born with the genetic caretaker personality, we will seek to attach ourselves to caretakees to take care of. If we have a talent in music, arts, athletics, we attach to our talent. Philosophy, science, religion, politics also offer avenues of attachment.

For example, if you are born with a personality that is very good at organizing things, you may use it to try to control your life. This control becomes, in its way, a form of attachment. However, in my opinion, we seek these attachments to relieve our fear of abandonment. We may encounter attachments that give us a brief sense of euphoria, which offers a false attachment in that it does not provide a healthy source of support to the person. Examples are alcohol and drug abuse, over-eating, pathological gambling, and hoarding objects, among others.

Sometimes people can hurt others because of their attachments. For example, a woman was complaining to me that her husband spent too much of his free time with his sports buddies. The woman and her children were being cheated. His possible over-attachment to his childhood sports buddies was helpful to him; however, it was not compatible with the obligations of a husband and father.

Often people are not aware of how much they are attached to objects. They may not realize the intensity of the attachment until they lose it, especially if the attachment to an object negatively affects attachments to other humans.

There are many attachments that can give temporary satisfaction. The following is an example. A middle-aged, married woman with children said to me one day in therapy, "I have a secret." She was gambling compulsively on slot machines. When I asked her what she was thinking during the gambling, she replied, "At the slot machine, there is no other world. I am not worried about anything. I am free from the world." It was an unhealthy attachment. As soon as she left the slot machine, her guilt and anger about damaging the family finances set in and depressed her.

Ideally an attachment should help a person in the struggle of life and not hurt anyone else. The best attachments in the world are bonded relationships with other human beings. The loss of any attachment possibly engenders anger at the loss. The greater the emotional attachment, the greater the pain of loss. Unfortunately, we are capable of attaching ourselves to the affect, or feeling, of anger, which I explore later. Our lives are filled with attachments and losses. How we recognize and deal with them is the history of our lives.

Chapter 7

Aggression and Anger

Early in my psychiatric practice, I realized that some patients suffering from anxiety, depression, psychosomatic symptoms, etc., were in stressful life situations that caused them to be more angry than they consciously realized. I further noticed that if they were able to extricate themselves from the stressful experience, often their symptoms improved and went into remission. I postulated that in the untenable life situation, the anger increased until it reached the level at which it could affect the neurotransmitters and produce symptoms. That postulated level of anger required to affect the neurotransmitters would, of course, have individual variations.

Many times, anger is generated by overwhelming stress on the job. At other times anger is generated by the stress of having to provide unreasonable emotional or other support to family or friends. At still other times, a loss of a very strong attachment can cause anger, especially if it is sudden and unanticipated.

In the relatively recent years of my ongoing practice of psychiatry, I became concerned that the affect (or feeling) of anger is increasing in our society. Patients and friends have expressed that same concern. There may be some statistical studies that would refute or confirm this.

Perhaps a definition of the affect, or feeling, of anger and aggression and opinions from other writers will be helpful. I am anticipating some readers will be less knowledgeable about psychoanalysis and would therefore prefer a definition of anger and aggression from the dictionary than a psychoanalytic glossary.

Aggression is defined in the Webster's *New World College Dictionary* (2014, p. 27), as forceful, attacking behavior, either constructively self-assertive and self-protective or destructively hostile to oneself or others. In the same dictionary (p. 54), *anger* is described as a feeling of displeasure resulting from injury, mistreatment, opposition, etc., and usually showing itself in a desire to fight back at the supposed cause of the feeling.

In this book we discuss anger as a feeling or an affect. We think of aggression as a behavior that can be destructive to oneself or others as a result of anger. Some psychoanalysts accept aggression as an instinctual drive derived from the unconscious and perhaps given equal status to the instinctual sexual drive. Freud did not originally consider aggression to be an instinctual drive but later changed his mind, particularly after the tremendous loss of life in World War I.

In psychoanalytic theory, instinctual drives derive from the unconscious mind putting pressure on the conscious mind to respond to them with behavior for better or worse. In this book, I do not attempt to debate the issue of whether or not there is an instinctual aggressive drive. I am content to deal with the affect or feeling of anger and how it impacts our personal lives, perhaps also our culture and even world events.

I would like to very briefly review some of the authors who have written about aggression. Alfred Adler believed that the drive for superiority or mastery and the inferiority complex that could result were more important than the unconscious dynamics put forth by Freud (Ellenberger, 1970). However, Henri Ellenberger in *The Discovery of the Unconscious* (1970) argued that the exiled Adler's influence was felt in Freud's eventual introduction of aggression into his own theoretical framework with the dual instinct theory.

Although Freud was more engaged with the exploration of the sexual drive, I would like to present briefly several of his thoughts on the aggressive drive.

> ***In all that follows I adopt the standpoint, therefore, that the inclination to aggression is an original, self-subsisting instinctual disposition in man, and I return to my view [p. 112] that it constitutes the greatest impediment to civilization.***
> *(Strachey & Freud, 1961, p. 122).*

Some corroboration of my contention that the repressed anger can be the generator of anxiety is described in Freud's case of "Little Hans," a child who repressed his aggressive tendencies, including hostility toward his parents. At the time, Freud thought Adler had erred in determining aggression as common to instinctual life and key to the understanding of psychological problems. However, many years later Freud himself postulated an instinct of aggression, albeit one very different from Adler's (Strachey & Freud, 1961). Near the end of his life, Freud expressed his thoughts on aggression to Marie Bonaparte:

To Marie Bonaparte. May 27, 1937

Meine liebe Marie:

I will try to answer your question (about aggression). The whole topic has not yet been treated carefully, and what I had to say about it in earlier writings was so premature and casual as hardly to deserve consideration (Jones, 1957, p. 464).

In the understanding of aggression, additional work has been done by researchers such as Melanie Klein, a lay analyst; Dr. Daniel S. Nagin at Carnegie Mellon University; and Richard Tremblay at the University of Montreal. Klein's work with very young children found that the internal world of very small children is full of destructive fantasies (Klein, 2002). Nagin and Tremblay concluded that the most aggressive boys are the 2- to 3-year-olds, the toddlers (Roth, 2006).

Some psychoanalysts believe in an aggressive instinct. A contrary opinion is expressed by Lumsden and Wilson (1963) in their book, *Promethean Fire*, in which they argue that:

Aggressive behavior is opportunistic, tending to evolve into certain forms that appear and are shaped genetically according to the particular needs of the species [p.33].

What I would like to emphasize from the work of the above-mentioned researchers is that anger is present in children early in life. In the next chapter, I propose a theory of how anger continues to be a powerful force in our lives.

Chapter 8

Possible Pathways to Deal with Anger

Differences between individuals and among groups are fertile ground for the expression of anger. Most often marriage presents a relationship between a caretaker and a caretakee. I will not repeat the list of personality characteristics of each; they are described in Chapter 1. Suffice it to say that a caretaker is one with more empathy for others and the caretakee has less empathy for others. A possible interaction is as follows:

> A caretaker complains to a caretakee with the question, "Why don't you once and for all clean up your dirty dishes that you left in the TV room last night?" The caretakee retorts, "Why does it bother you? If you don't like it, clean it up yourself." The caretaker responds, "You always have some excuse for your laziness." The caretakee replies, "You always think you are so perfect."

These arguments can go on endlessly as the anger mounts, and nothing worthwhile is going to come out of the interaction between them. It is fair to say that the caretakee often leaves things to be picked up by the caretaker. This is a typical passive-aggressive behavior that, in essence, says *take care of me, pick up after me.* This is the caretakee's way of saying "You should mother me."

The caretaker is not without blame. His anger at having to put up with the caretakee's passive-aggressive behavior encouraged him to express his criticism in an angry tone, which he may not be conscious of. He should have been more diplomatic in his request. He could have said, "Dear, it would be a big help to me if you would remember to bring the dishes to the kitchen when you leave the TV room and head to bed." It may not solve the problem, but it might keep the caretaker from getting into an angry argument with the caretakee.

Also, according to my hypothesis, both caretaker and caretakee are, to some extent, attached consciously and unconsciously to anger. Therefore, unless one resolves not to allow his attachment to anger cause a verbal fight, it will continue. Usually it is the caretaker who will have to decide not to let his anger provoke further anger, even when the caretakee is provoking anger in him. It will be hard for the caretaker to do that because his attachment to his anger is also strong.

The attachment to anger by both individuals is related to their fear of abandonment. I think the best chance of having a meaningful discussion is for one partner to refuse to initiate or return the anger he feels. If there is any chance of the caretakee changing his passive-aggressive approach, it will be because the caretaker has refused to engage in an angry response. I have seen this work in patients and friends. No matter what the issue, when either partner introduces anger, communication suffers and issues are difficult to resolve.

Attempting to gain control of our anger is often difficult. We are attached to it for emotional security. We don't want to be abandoned in this world. However, we carry guilt about the anger that can be conscious, unconscious, or both. In either case, we may punish ourselves by being careless and causing injury to ourselves, or possibly by provoking others to harm us or attacking our immune system and causing physical illness. More importantly, when we succumb to angry exchanges we lose the opportunity to bond with others, which could lead to a more healthy and pleasurable self-image for both parties.

Each time we prevent ourselves from returning the anger we are setting an example that might be followed by others. In each encounter with our fellow human beings, we have an opportunity to decline bringing anger to the interaction and perhaps have an opportunity to relate to another in an empathetic way that generates respect and confidence in each. This type of "psychological growth," as Thomas Ogden described it, "involves a form of self-acceptance that can be achieved only in the context of a real relationship with a relatively psychologically mature person" (Gabbard et al., 2012, p. 182). I believe the caretaker personality with humility is perhaps the best one to initiate the communication in the direction of bonding. Obviously it won't always work, but that shouldn't keep us from trying. It might be helpful to remember the words of Albert Schweitzer, who is widely quoted as saying, "Example is not the main thing in influencing others. It is the only thing."

Chapter 9

Hypotheses

Edward O. Wilson and Daniel C. Dennett (2010) wrote that: "...if you believe that the brain is not a blank slate, that there are deeply embedded programs of prepared learning that guide people in their mental development, then it makes sense to try to understand the deep history of humanity." This statement supports my hypotheses on anger and attachment.

Stated briefly, a hypothesis is a theory, something not proven at the time but perhaps proven or discarded in the future. We do know that sometime in our past we evolved the state of consciousness, which meant that we were no longer driven by our instincts alone. We became able to think about our existence and how vulnerable we are, not only from the forces of nature but also at the hands of our fellow human beings.

I believe the affect of anger stimulated us to be aggressive in defense of ourselves and so benefitted our survival as a species. Possibly, the affect of anger supplied the psychic energy that allows the ego to repress painful life experiences, removing them from the conscious mind to the unconscious mind. Possibly we developed a greater attachment to anger because it lessened our fear of abandonment. Being abandoned would mean not having any supporting attachments in life.

Over time, we developed guilt about our anger, which also could be repressed by the ego. Thus, we could develop both conscious and unconscious attachments to anger and guilt about the attachments. This guilt may also carry a conscious and unconscious need to be punished (Auchincloss & Glick, 1996, p. 15).

Another hypothetical consideration is that the attachment to anger is in a rivalry with the attachment to bonding, which also is in our genetic make-up because it also helped the survival of the species. When the attachment to anger is operating between two people or groups, it prevents the opportunity to attach ourselves in a meaningful relationship that could lead to bonding. Attachments to bonding benefit both partners by giving each person in the relationship positive conscious and unconscious images of themselves. When the attachment to anger is operating between two people or groups of people, it diminishes the possibility of solving any dispute between them. My central hypothesis, therefore, is that the attachment to anger, the attachment to bonding, the personalities of the caretaker and caretakee, and the fear of abandonment are all in our genetic make-up.

Chapter 10

In Closing

In previous chapters I have presented hypotheses that will be accepted or rejected over time. The hypotheses address our attachment to anger, attachment to bonding, caretaker personalities and caretakee personalities, and our fear of abandonment. These forces operate in our daily lives with little or no insight that they are effecting our behavior. The attachment to anger increases in proportion to the decrease in bonding. Conversely, the increase in bonding reduces the attachment to anger.

In our daily lives, there are many opportunities to refrain from anger but our attachment to anger thwarts us. We have to make a stronger effort to recognize it and deal with it in a more constructive manner.

One final thought: If we could transfer the psychic energy of anger to the act of bonding with others, would it enable us to build a stronger and more productive society?

PART 2
Case Studies

Case Study 1

This patient, a middle-aged woman, was admitted to the hospital in a semi-comatose state after being found by her mother. She had taken an overdose of prescription medications (prescribed by her family doctor) along with a considerable amount of alcohol. Previously, she drank only at social occasions.

When I entered her hospital room for the consultation, I saw five close family members at her bedside. My first impression was that it was wonderful to see such a supportive family, which would be helpful in her treatment. I could not have been more wrong.

She gave a history of at least one depression, approximately twenty years prior, brought on by the death of her father and the stress of a job change. She complained that treatment by a previous psychiatrist had not helped, but she had recovered in about six to eight months with the help of a priest.

The patient described herself as a homebody with no outside interests. She had never married or even dated. Her social friendships were limited. She did enjoy, to some extent, the friendship of fellow workers on some jobs. Despite being a high school graduate, she believed her intelligence was limited. Whatever her limitations may have been, she was an excellent worker and very demanding of herself.

During the years I treated her, she relied on my help to keep her psychologically sound. However, while she accepted the insights she gained from the treatments, she couldn't allow herself to act on them. She was rigid in her adherence to her caretaker role within her family, even though other members made no commitment to her other than using her for their own selfish needs.

She described her mother as a somewhat limited caretaker who could be very critical of her if she didn't perform her household chores perfectly. Her mother's desire for perfection and tendency to hoard were, in my opinion, indicative of the mother's own insecurities.

Perhaps the father could be described as the most emotionally needy of them all. He was extremely dependent on his own mother and, for a time, left his wife and my patient early in her life. When he returned to the marriage, other siblings were born.

As I tried in treatment to understand the underlying struggle causing her emotional pain, I came to the conclusion that my patient was
never able to separate herself from the role of caretaker. Her sense
of self-worth was predicated on maintaining that role. Furthermore,
I believe the family had inculcated in her the idea that her only duty
in life was to give of herself to the other members of the family. At
least some caretakers get an occasional "thank you." That was not
the case with her relatives. The other members of the family were
determined to keep her under their control, so she never developed
the sense of self-worth and independence that come from relationships that consider each person's needs in a joint communication
endeavor.

In my patient's life, her family's demands were automatically set
in motion. The patient complied with their requests, no matter how
unreasonable and selfish they were. For example, one sibling had
no hesitancy in insisting that my patient be on call if she needed a
babysitter. There was never a discussion or a respectful request, it
was just understood that my patient was there to serve her. When
my patient was seriously ill and requested some help, it was given
reluctantly or refused entirely. The selfishness never paused. It was
ongoing not only by one family member but by all of them.

Another sibling just as selfishly insisted that the patient act as her
chauffeur or let her use the patient's car at will, even though she was
working and could easily afford a car. The sibling never offered any
money to cover the cost of gas or other expenses. Yet another family
member would disturb the patient by calling her at home without any
regard of the time or whether it was disturbing the patient's sleep.
She also tried to sell the patient a car, which she could no longer
drive, at an inflated price. It didn't make any difference that my patient
had a car and didn't need another.

These examples are only a few of the countless demands the
patient experienced over time. The family members were angry with
me because they knew my treatment was designed to free her of
being used and come to terms with how much the repressed anger
was causing her to feel guilty and therefore even more angry.

The consequence of that anger – at being so exploited – was the primary reason she was suffering from anxiety, depression, and the obsessive ruminations that would cause her to visit the clergyman or petition me to prescribe better medications as well as give support similar to that of the clergyman.

The patient's attempts to assuage her anxiety and depression by overeating led to obesity and metabolic problems. If, on occasion, she became physically ill, her family members would become worried and solicitous. But as soon as she got well, they went back to their usual exploitation of her. The motto of my patient's family seemed to be, "Don't ask me what I can do for you, just do whatever I ask as soon as I ask it."

Near the end of my contact with her, the patient had begun treatment for a serious illness. At the same time, she was being pressured to leave her home and live with another relative. I believed that such a move would only exacerbate her emotional distress. In retrospect, I believe she was going to make the move. However, she broke off treatment at that time and I believe she transferred her considerable anger over the years of being exploited by her family onto me and rejected me instead of refusing to be taken advantage of by her family.

I continued to be concerned about her physical as well as her emotional health. I tried to contact several family members to get an update, but they never returned my calls. Eventually, my staff showed me an obituary listing for my patient. I can only wonder whether the ongoing stress and anger she experienced turned inward and weakened her immune system.

This case study demonstrates how powerful unhealthy attachments can be. Some life attachments promote a sense of well-being, while others promote anger. I believe the anger engendered daily by the repeated exploitation of the self accumulates, and a reservoir of unhealthy, even toxic, attachments and anger is built up over time.

I presented this case to illustrate how much resistance to change can be present in our lives. Most psychiatrists, psychoanalysts, and therapists would agree. People are reluctant to give up some attachments, no matter how much they suffer from them. Change is difficult because it is hard to give up one attachment for a better one, unless you can trust it.

Everyone is afraid to be alone to some extent; some more than others. What helps to relieve that fear is having enough healthy attachments with others who want a relationship that shares empathy, honesty, respect, trust, and genuine hope. I have come to believe that if a change for a better relationship is going to happen over time, the initiation will more than likely have to come from the caretaker. It is the worn-out caretaker who comes to see me rather than the caretakee. ▦

Case Study 2

In many histories, caretakees attempt to exploit a caretaker. But sometimes caretakees attempt to exploit each other. The following history is another example of how family members can make a patient become emotionally ill.

The patient was in her 60s and referred to me by her family doctor after he had hospitalized her for gastrointestinal symptoms and could find no physical reason for her symptoms. She was happily married with an emotionally supportive husband and daughter.

In her first interview, she described herself as being depressed for the first time in her life, which her husband corroborated. For several years prior to the onset of the depression, she and her husband witnessed one of her siblings taking financial advantage of the other siblings. My patient tended to ignore how much she was being taken advantage of, and she never took legal action because she couldn't handle confrontation with anyone. Her family saw her as weak and gullible.

Approximately six months after our first meeting, my patient was admitted to a psychiatric unit for worsening depression. The husband had to get an attorney to make it clear he didn't want her family to visit after the nurse informed him that his wife became agitated after her family visited.

My patient did well for several years after that hospitalization. But she gradually became depressed again and her husband noted that it seemed to correlate with frequent visits from her family. After another hospitalization, she was once again in remission, which lasted for several years. Incidentally, I did not treat her in the hospital, but I was in contact with her psychiatrist.

Undue stress returned when the company she was working for offered a severance package. This seemingly attractive cash sum, in the opinion of her boss, her husband, and myself, was not as good as her forthcoming retirement package. Her family began to pressure her to take the severance sum, which would then make her new-found cash available for them to try to use. The patient could not deal with the pressure and she decompensated, becoming agitated and depressed and requiring hospitalization again. She left the hospital after two days because her mother told her she didn't have to stay. She required another subsequent hospitalization for electrolyte imbalance caused by drinking excessive amounts of water, but she recovered in the intensive care unit without complication.

After six months, she was readmitted to the hospital once more. At the same time, her husband reported to the police that expensive jewelry, which also had sentimental attachments, was stolen from their home. After the report, some of the jewelry was magically returned to the home. The husband believed the police report was the stimulus for the return of some of the articles. The husband also suspected that he had discovered the theft too late, and some of the items had already been fenced. The robbery occurred when both the husband and patient were working. The patient's family had keys to the house at the time. Their keys have since been taken away. There have been no burglaries since then. All of this led the husband to believe the family had committed the thefts.

At the time of this writing, the patient has been well for several years. She followed good advice and did not take the severance package. With the help of her boss, she was able to secure the retirement package she had earned. Her husband has made it clear that she must stay away from her family and they are not to ever visit them. Otherwise, he has informed the patient he will divorce her and move away. So far, she understands and is complying with his wishes and is maintaining remission of her depression.

In summary, this is another example of how some people in a family can exploit another member's weaknesses (i.e. fear of confrontation and emotional dependency on others). The patient's family had not the slightest remorse in their selfishness. I regret not recognizing the problem earlier. I assumed the depression was brought on by work stress when, in retrospect, it was not. It was the family repeatedly calling her at work and urging her to leave her husband and live with them. They knew precisely her weaknesses and were intent on exploiting them. Her husband and I were not aware of these damaging, stressful calls. The patient was very much in denial about her feelings and her husband was far too passive in his approach to helping early in her treatment. My treatment helped him be less passive, and he partnered more in her treatment. Unfortunately, there will be an ongoing need to protect her from the stress laid on her by the family. Without her husband and their adult child's vigilance and support, she remains vulnerable to exploitation by the family now and possibly by others in the future.

In her childhood search for emotional support, the patient allowed herself to be used. She was a caretakee in a family of multiple caretakees. Unfortunately, she married a caretaker husband who initially was not strong or knowledgeable enough of her family to be a help to her. I was able to elicit his help to become a stronger caretaker for his wife, and this has contributed to the remission of her depression.

I have encouraged the patient to try to develop a supportive group through a group activity, and she did so at one time. It was enjoyable and good for her self-confidence. However, she has not continued to avail herself of that support. As of this writing she remains symptom free, but if she is once again exposed to exploitation of her family members, I feel that she will certainly become depressed again. ▪

Case Study 3

This single woman in her 40s was referred to me by her family doctor. Her chief complaint was, "I need help learning to deal with anxiety attacks." The anxiety started in high school, and she did get relief from counseling with a psychologist. In response, she gradually made friends who supported her emotionally.

Her anxiety returned after she started college. She resumed counseling with a previous psychologist, but she didn't feel that she received enough help and particularly complained of the psychologist's treatment and too frequent absences. She had been prescribed an antidepressant and a tranquilizer by her family doctor, which I continued to prescribe for her.

The patient's family history indicated psychological stresses. I had previously treated her father for anxiety attacks. She was the youngest of several siblings. She remembered feeling psychologically supported by only one male sibling. She feared for her life at times because another male sibling became aggressive when inebriated and threatened members of the family, although he never acted on his threats. In general, the patient described her life at home as one of fending off teasing by the older siblings. When she became emotionally upset, they told her she would lose control and "go crazy."

Early on in treatment with me, the patient was able to gain back the weight she had lost and was experiencing no problem with sleep or appetite. She openly expressed confidence in me because I rarely cancelled an appointment. As a result, she became emotionally attached to me almost immediately.

Her anxiety waxed and waned according to any loss of emotional support from family, friends, or significant others. I learned that it was not just the fear of a loss of support that troubled her. In fact, she was unreasonably afraid that she would be thought insane and put away. When her boyfriend first asked her to move in with him, she declined. However, after much thought, she decided to accept his invitation to move in together. It became obvious to me, and later to her, that he was not any better at emotional support than her family.

In my opinion, the patient was born with a caretaker personality.

She was often called upon by family members to do an errand for them or babysit their children. Unfortunately, she was used by them and didn't receive enough gratitude for the help that she provided them. Her father would frequently elicit her help on weekends to go to a store with him and then send her into the store alone to purchase what goods he wanted. She was so short, she could hardly reach the counter. He would remain in the car until she returned with the purchases. I assume this was at the time when he was experiencing his own anxiety.

Fortunately for my patient, she had the ability to make friends. These friendships were almost always positive for her. In addition, she also benefited from her intelligence and love of learning, which led to a college degree and professional life. I believe she attached herself to these things and they made her feel good about herself.

Attachments are potentially everywhere, and people use them to sustain themselves emotionally.

An example of how attachments can have a subtle effect on people: The patient's boyfriend had been away one weekend, and she was comfortably alone on a Sunday morning. She arose and fixed breakfast, made herself a cup of tea, and leisurely read the newspaper. After this, she cleaned up the breakfast table and suddenly had an anxiety attack. When I saw her the next day, she was anxious and puzzled by the experience.

After exploring the circumstances surrounding the previous day, I realized that her Sunday morning ritual usually revolved around her school assignments for the next week. But she had no assignments for the coming week because the semester was over. This could seem too simple an explanation, but the patient was able to use the insight and feel less anxious. This insight allowed her to see how she sought attachments, for better or worse, depending on whether they are supporting or destructive to her sense of self-worth.

At the time, not enough positive attachments were forthcoming in her marriage. Fortunately, she and her husband have since had a child. This gives my patient the possibility of a better attachment than she has with her husband, who is repeatedly disrespectful and critical of her. Although, at times, he doesn't hesitate to call on her professional and expert advice in matters where their particular fields merge. These requests are not followed with a sincere and heartfelt praise.

She is a caretaker and he is a caretakee. She is more likely to empathize in her relationships with others, more emotionally tuned-in to other people, and quick to observe others' needs for help; whereas he is, in many ways, too selfish to extend himself to her.

For example, they were on an outing in the summer with their school-aged child. The day was particularly hot, and my patient became dehydrated. She experienced a migraine headache, heat exhaustion, and considerable nausea, which led to vomiting. She was very much in need of someone to provide water, help her get to a cooler place, and provide emotional support. Her husband took their child and left her where she was. Later, strangers approached her and offered help and she called me for medical advice and emotional support.

In another example, the school-aged daughter was emotionally upset one evening as she contemplated a necessary change in schools, which would result in the possible loss of good friends. She was nauseous and became terrified that she might vomit. After witnessing the girl's extreme distress, my patient's husband told their daughter to get a hold of herself or she would become "crazy like her mother."

In contrast, my patient took the girl to a bedroom where they held each other tightly while lying in bed, which made the child feel reassured. Their daughter then fell asleep with no recurrence of her distress. Incidentally, the child had witnessed the mother's helpless state and vomiting on the prior outing. What the child may have gathered from that incident is that if you get nauseated and vomit, no one will come to your rescue.

What are the consequences of this less-than-well-functioning marriage? Certainly, my patient is replaying the search for emotional support from a husband because she didn't get enough of it in her childhood. Unfortunately, now she is challenged to get emotional support from a husband who would rather critically control her than build her up. The dilemma is that neither one wants to be alone. He is afraid if he supports her emotionally, she will get stronger and leave him. She is afraid if she doesn't put up with his behavior, he will leave her. They are each afraid of abandonment by the other.

This same husband, who is an unashamed bully to his wife, doesn't have the courage to go up against his father who dominates him. Recently, he lost a close friend. At the memorial service that he and his wife attended, he became so distraught that he had to place his hand on her thigh to reassure himself. My patient gradually realized her husband is a paper tiger, but she is too afraid to be alone, so her challenges to his attempts to dominate are not as strong as needed. She has repeatedly asked him to join us in our treatment sessions, but he has repeatedly declined by stating, "She is the one who is crazy." What I have described in him is typically seen in many caretakees.

The fear of abandonment is not the only cause of my patient's anxiety. She was born with a personality that likes organization and perfection. In my opinion, she used this attribute of her personality to organize the world around her. This gave her a sense of security. However, if she couldn't organize something that was important to her, the problem then became too burdensome and she, of course, was unable to feel good about herself and became anxious. She agreed, however, that that kind of anxiety is easier to handle than the terrifying thought of abandonment.

Accompanying this fear of abandonment is the affect of anger. I believe that built up anger can reach the point where it affects the neurotransmitters, resulting in anxiety and depression, among other disorders.

Maybe you are asking, "So what is the answer, doctor?" It is, as its center point, the anger of neglect that gets played out in many ways.

Recently, my patient was employed in her chosen field and a wonderful experience ensued. In contrast to the way she was being treated at home, she was accepted by her co-workers. They respected her professionally and frequently asked her for help. She was perplexed because she had never been treated this well in her life. It added another measure of confidence in herself and reduced her anxiety even further. Unfortunately, she was let go when the company requested she do something that she considered unethical and she refused. Despite the firing, she continues to benefit from the experience. She has received many calls from the people who befriended her and are angry that she is no longer there. Fortunately, she has recently found another job where she is appreciated.

What she experienced at work was a healing relationship. A healing relationship embodies certain characteristics. First is an empathic respect for each other's emotional needs. This does not mean that each person has to meet the other's emotional needs, but that there is an understanding of each other's needs and an honest exchange in that regard. Another important aspect is that each person does not allow the interaction between them to incorporate an angry exchange. Anger destroys the opportunity to bring about a healthy relationship.

What I have just described in a relationship is just the opposite of what my patient experienced in her relationship with her husband. The destructiveness of the husband's highly critical, angry, apathetic behaviors may well cause a separation and impel my patient to seek more healthy relationships.

Not only is the husband's behavior destructive to my patient, but she has to intervene on their daughter's behalf to prevent psychological damage to the child. The girl, nearing the end of grade school, is showing some talent in both athletics and music. The husband is highly critical of her if she doesn't exert herself in what he considers proper practice. It is clear that he never exerted himself and only wants to vicariously enjoy her talent. His driving her to greater practice and success is only for his vicarious needs. He has no insight into his destructive selfishness. Luckily my patient is poised to intervene any time she sees the beginning of another episode. Also, the child quickly responds to my patient's empathy and protection, reducing any potential psychological damage.

Again, people can make people sick.

Case Study 4

A woman in her in her 60s came to see me because her husband asked her to see a psychiatrist. He believed that she had a severe personality disorder. She had been experiencing some difficulty initiating and maintaining sleep. In addition, her mood would fluctuate. At various times she experienced depression, anxiety, or stress-induced somatic symptoms.

She had been referred by her family doctor, who had placed her on an antidepressant, which I changed due to side effects. I also added a small dose of a tranquilizer to be taken only when needed and a non-addicting sleep aid.

The patient was the youngest of several siblings. I had treated her mother very briefly some years prior for stress-induced mood symptoms brought on by one of the patient's siblings, who dominated the mother. Her father was deceased and may well have suffered from alcohol abuse. Possibly he was on the bipolar spectrum. The patient had been married for 10 years, and neither she nor her husband were previously married. She had a high school diploma, some college courses, an excellent work ethic, and was employed as an office worker.

As we worked together in psychotherapy, it became apparent that she was being stressed by her family, her marriage, and some other social relationships. One sibling was unreasonably dominating the mother, who then went to my patient for support in dealing with the sibling. For example, the patient and her husband had given her mother some money. When the patient learned that the sibling managed to get money from the mother, coupled with the mother's inability to deal with that sibling (which I knew of from treating her years ago), it caused a problem. The mother relied on my patient to listen to her problems with the older sibling.

The caretaker-patient was not initially aware of how she was being used, nor did she have insight as to how angry she was because of it. Her mood fluctuated in accordance with how much stress emanated from within her family, her husband, and her employment. Early on, she saw herself as being at the mercy of these stressful relationships. She felt powerless to change and her self-esteem and self-confidence suffered.

Approximately one year into the treatment, she brought her husband to a session. It became obvious that the only reason he came was to convince me that his wife had a personality disorder, which I was not diagnosing. He then became angry with me and never returned to another session. He did write several days later apologizing for "blowing up," but maintained the same logic in regard to his diagnosis of his wife and my lack of understanding of it. Since he was not successful in convincing me, he turned to other professionals and to the clergy. To the best of my and his wife's knowledge, he convinced no one but himself.

Other manifestations blatantly showed his childish, manipulative behavior. He gradually became aware that my work with the patient was making it more difficult for him to control her. In addition to not talking, he would declare that he would not eat food she prepared. This never lasted very long, but early on it often had a devastating effect on my patient. However, as she gained insight to his ongoing need to control her with repeated negative comments about her, she began to see how it all started early in her life.

Although she was the most sensitive and empathic in her family, she got little recognition for it, even though others depended on her for support. She realized she was frequently made to feel guilty and gained very little positive emotional support. Gradually, she saw the same conflicts were present in her marriage. Her husband wanted to keep her by domination and control. He was not able to love her in a way that would make both of them feel good about themselves, and he had no faith in interacting with her as a grownup. Her husband was stuck in his own development with the immature and manipulative behavior of a child.

My patient has come to understand the dynamics of her self-effacing posture in regard to others. Most importantly, she is more aware of how much repressed anger is engendered by allowing others to use her and give little in return. She sees more clearly the relationship between her psychological symptoms and the repressed anger, and she is beginning to change the way she relates to others, which will not only help her but possibly others around her as well. If they could see that she will not allow herself to be psychologically abused by them, they might reconsider their behavior toward her or just stay away from her. The patient could be the person to bring about that change.

Caretakees are not able or willing to initiate a change in how they relate to others, but confident caretakers can set changes into motion, resulting in either positive emotional support or a departure from the relationship.

At one point the patient's anger, although disguised to some extent, was obviously directed at me. When I pointed this out, she was able to elaborate on it and gained some insight that has been helpful for her. In essence, I said, "You are angry because I'm not providing enough psychological relief to you in our treatment." She accepted this insight and realized she didn't have to feel guilty about her anger. She also understood that I had no need to punish her for being angry with me. I wanted her to see that when she was rejected by others, it was understandable that she would be angry. Pent up anger at being used by others was causing the fluctuations in her mood. She was not being paranoid when she described the behavior of certain others (i.e. her husband, her family, or other social relationships).

Fortunately, the patient had a few social relationships that nourished and enriched her emotionally. She learned how to avoid relationships that did not enhance her own self-esteem and self-confidence, and she began to maximize relations that did provide that. Because of this progress, her mental state gradually improved.

During her treatment I realized that she might suffer from attention deficit disorder. She previously was not aware of it. A trial of medication made a great deal of difference and added to her confidence at work. A repetitive dream of many years in which she entered a room and couldn't find her way out became less frightening to her.

I had not seen the patient for several months when she called with an urgent plea to see me as soon as possible. She was very depressed, anxious, and felt like she had lost all that she had gained emotionally in her therapy. She had not been to work for two days and had rid herself of a psychological counselor, recommended by her employer, who had not been helpful. She apologized for not calling sooner, possibly because she didn't want me to see her failing to keep the improvements she had gained.

The precipitating event that distressed her was caused by a coworker, somewhat senior to her in rank. My patient was sitting at her desk, working on a particular work problem, when the coworker, who was always finding ways to use my patient as a sounding board for her own emotional stresses but at the same time was very angry, controlling, and highly critical, gave her something to look at. The coworker's behavior was intrusive. My patient accepted the rather insignificant thing and returned to her work. The coworker, who was standing over my patient, then yelled, "You are not paying attention to me." At first, my patient thought the coworker was not serious, but when it continued, my patient broke down emotionally and was afraid to return to work.

What we were able to understand by going over the encounter was that her success in therapy enabled my patient to relate to others with a pleasure and confidence that her attacking coworker viewed with envy and anger. With that insight in place, her emotional confidence returned and she knew she could return to work and handle the situation. I also pointed out how she could alert others in authority to the problem if that coworker continued to demean her or make the workplace unhealthy for her.

At the time of this writing, the patient believes she has more control of her own life and likes it. Instead of being at the mercy of others who want to drain her emotionally and control her, she feels freer to make her own decisions without feeling guilty. By refusing to allow herself to be drawn into arguments perpetuated by others, she moves on to find others who enhance her self-esteem. She is now more relaxed and better able to enjoy her life. Her family and husband now have a more happy and confident person who will not allow the problems of others to make her sick.

These new relationships build self-esteem and self-confidence. Those old relationships that brought on angry exchanges did not. ■

Case Study 5

A female patient, in her early 30s and not married, sought psychiatric help for being "high strung," nervous, and anxious. There was no previous history of psychiatric treatment, even though there were previous episodes of emotional distress.

She was, at the time of the first session with me, working in the mental health field with a very difficult group of patients who caused her considerable stress. She stated, "I hate my job." She was not sleeping well and was constantly fatigued. Her overeating because of all of the above resulted in unwanted weight.

More distressing to her were some obsessive thoughts and behaviors. For example, she believed she might have lost notes on patients and repeatedly returned to her desk to make sure she had not lost them. In addition, she was overly concerned that while driving, would strike a pothole, for instance, and might strike a pedestrian.

I strongly recommended that she seek a transfer to a less onerous job, which fortunately she was able to do. As a result, her symptoms subsided considerably in just two weeks, and she reported, "I'm not biting people's heads off." She further stated that the job change "lifted a load off" her. Her family agreed. She had also been prescribed an antidepressant, but it was highly unlikely that the antidepressant could have worked that rapidly. Getting out of the overwhelmingly stressful job provided more cogent relief.

As we explored her life history, the patient remembered being extremely attached to her mother and that it had been difficult for her to start school because of her fear of losing her mother. At age 17, she worked at the checkout counter at a local business. On one occasion, a gentleman who was checking out put his purchase on the counter and a drop of his blood, which may have been from a cut, fell onto his package. My patient was immediately fearful that she would be infected with his germs. This is still a sensitive issue with her. She is admittedly germ-conscious. This unfortunate incident seemed to coincide with her unrecognized fear and anger about going away to college and having to give up old friends and struggle to find new ones.

She has been my patient exclusively for almost two decades.

During this time, she could remain relatively asymptomatic for several years at a time and be without medication for the same period. The exacerbation of her symptoms has almost invariably correlated with being trapped in a job situation. However, loss of her dog and loss of a favorite grandparent also brought on some anxiety.

During therapy, it became apparent to me that she was very well liked by most people and also that she was a caretaker. She was a person who liked to be helpful to others. Her sense of well-being and confidence in herself depended on her taking care of others. In addition to the caretaking characteristic, she was also born with a controlling personality, feeling the need to organize things in her life to make herself feel good. All of us grow up using whatever personality traits we have to relate to others, and hopefully we experience some positive feelings because we are being appreciated. When we don't get the desired result, we get angry and, depending on a person's chemistry, it can trigger neurotransmitters and result in symptoms such as anxiety, depression, and psychosomatic symptoms, among others.

As therapists, we have not taken into account enough of what a powerful force anger can be. Whenever there is even a slight rejection to our sense of well-being, there is some degree of anger depending on the circumstances.

To be more specific, in this patient's life she had no control of the stress and no one to appeal to. She was becoming angrier because it was impossible to take good care of her patients. Her sense of her own self-worth was going down the drain, so to speak, and this contributed to a rising tide of anger.

Anger, much of which is unconscious, sets off obsessive thoughts and behavior. It is as though the ego is saying, "Since we can't control the anger, let's feel guilty about it. Let's obsess about controlling something else in our life. Maybe that will relieve it."

It is fair to say that controlling something else, like revisiting her desk repeatedly, is less dangerous to the ego than expressing her anger consciously and losing her job. Other ways the ego can respond is by saying, "Let's project the anger outward by worrying that we might kill someone accidentally," or, "Let's turn it inward and become depressed."

Another observation to consider is how much, in some cases, care-takees can take advantage of their caretakers by overloading them with work or personal requests.

A child with a caretaker personality can be exploited by other members of the family, even the parents. In my therapy with the patient, the mother depended more on my patient's emotional support to her than she possible could give to my patient. Therefore, my patient would have to be careful not to develop too close a bond with anyone else, so as not to suffer painfully (emotionally) if there were a separation.

Interestingly enough, the patient has had two meaningful relationships with boyfriends. The first boyfriend was too emotionally needy and the break-up with him did not disturb her. She then began living with another man who was less needy. The relationship is going well at the time of this writing. She is more the caretaker, but he is not as needy as the other gentleman.

At one point, I asked the patient if, since the relationship had been going well, there were any plans for marriage. She answered, "Oh my, no." She was quite content to enjoy the relationship indefinitely without committing herself to a bonding relationship – like she had with her mother – that would cause too much distress if it ended. My patient felt the insights we brought out in therapy gave her a better chance to protect herself emotionally.

She has reverted to symptoms only whenever she was caught in a job situation that caused uncontrollable anger and feelings of helplessness. At these times, the ego brought out a substitute attempt to deal with the anger and guilt about the anger through obsessive thinking and compulsive behaviors, all of which receded when the anger was relieved by a job change. She will, however, remain vulnerable to a return of her symptoms if she once again encounters a toxic situation she can't control that causes her an undue amount of anger.

Case Study 6

This female patient, in her late 40s and married for the second time, was experiencing symptoms of anxiety and depression, which began 15 years earlier, after her father died. Previously, she was helped by a Jungian-trained psychoanalyst. She believed her present anxiety to be similar to the anxiety she experienced when her father died. The patient and her two siblings were adopted. The father had been a very busy physician, and the patient was her mother's confidante, fitting the typical caretaker personality.

The patient's anxiety and depression improved with psychotherapy and medication. But her symptoms increased after her husband lost his job. He became more needy and dependent than usual. She was frustrated by the increasing workload she was experiencing, with no relief in sight. At the time, she was seeing a psychologist for therapy and I was prescribing the medications. She was becoming more aware of the husband's caretakee personality, reflected in his undue selfishness with her and their child.

After a four-year gap in which I did not see her, the patient returned to treatment with me and gave a history of having divorced her husband and finding a boyfriend who was genuinely in love with her and who treated her respectfully. Although she was the caretaker, he was a cooperating caretakee and did not demand full attention at all times.

Unfortunately, her biggest worry was her daughter, who had attended college in another state, didn't do well, and was now living at home after leaving school and failing to find employment and a life of her own. The daughter had had a boyfriend at college who was emotionally supportive of her, but who, unfortunately, left school before she did. The daughter, understandably, resented her mother's boyfriend, even though he was kind and supportive to both of them. My patient and her daughter were in conflict. Her daughter appeared to be as needy emotionally as her father had been.

My patient continued to improve in psychotherapy. She began to see how many people depended on her emotionally. Like many caretakers, she never realized how valuable an asset that was for herself and others. She learned how to recognize when she was being exploited by others, which only caused anger and tripped her neurotransmitters to produce anxiety and depression. In addition to dealing with the problems with her daughter, she had to deal with the death of her stepfather. In spite of this, she was gaining insight into how she functioned psychologically and, though still stressed, was enjoying better coping skills and more confidence.

Although pleased that she was steadily improving, my patient was pained by the lack of improvement in her relationship with her daughter. She and I often reviewed the conversations between them. The patient was very willing to explore any issue with her daughter, but there appeared to be a stalemate.

Then suddenly, out of nowhere, there was a change in the daughter. She evolved from a very needy, selfish, angry, and stubborn caretakee (characteristics she shared with her father) and started showing the caretaker characteristics of her mother. My patient and I were stunned and skeptical that it would last, but it continued and even increased in quantity and quality.

To the daughter's benefit, she has entered a relationship with a very caring boyfriend and obviously gets emotional support from him. Although that relationship was helpful, it didn't seem to answer the question of the seemingly total change in the daughter.

The answer may have lain elsewhere, and my patient and I believed we found it. Approximately six months before, my patient was driving with her daughter in the passenger seat when they were struck by another car. There was no physical injury, but both mother and daughter had some brief post-traumatic stress. What is important is that my patient took charge, reassuring her daughter, handling the police report, dealing with the insurance company – things a caretaker mother does naturally without hesitation.

Not too long after that, the daughter had a scheduled cosmetic surgery. It was apparent to my patient and her daughter that the surgeon did not do exactly what he promised to do prior to the surgery. The daughter was naturally angry and sad about the experience. I encouraged my patient to meet with the surgeon and get an explanation as well as a solution to the problem. Here again, my patient took charge and, in resolving the distresses of her daughter, showed how strong and competent she could be.

This encouraged my patient and me to review the history of her relationship with her daughter, beginning in the daughter's childhood. My patient clearly recalls how distressed she was in the failure of her first marriage. The relationship with her husband was very damaging to her self-esteem and confidence. She often suffered from anxiety and depression, and she recollected clearly how her own conflicts kept her from being the supportive kind of mother she needed to be.

The daughter must have perceived her mother as weak and easily dominated by her father and this, perhaps, caused the daughter to identify with her caretakee-father more so than her caretaker-mother. Possibly, the daughter saw this kind of behavior that promotes more anger than healthy bonding as a way to get attention from her mother.

I believe it is fair to say that getting the patient to stop interacting with her child, as she acted with her husband, opened a new door for them. When my patient refused to argue, yet remained open to healthy bonding with her daughter, we began to see a change in the daughter. When the daughter saw her mother as strong and capable of protecting her, she allowed herself to identify with her and developed her own caretaker personality. In this case, the daughter was born with the caretaker personality, but it lay dormant because of the conflicts in the family that caused anxiety in the daughter and forced her to identify with the angry father. My patient and I felt hopeful that the change in the daughter would continue as it seems to be. ▪

Case Study 7

This female patient in her 30s was admitted voluntarily to the hospital on my service because of depression, which was seemingly precipitated by romantic failure and criticism by others of her behavior due to difficulty dealing with a divorced husband, an ex-common-law husband, and her lover.

She had a previous history of depression after divorcing her first husband. She was distraught enough to want to die but was not suicidal. After 12 days, she was discharged much improved and was followed at a community mental health facility in her area for the next five years.

Following her treatment through the community mental health facility, she returned to see me again and gave a history of being severely depressed for at least one month. She was afraid she would have to admit herself again despite being much improved. She wanted me to treat her. As had been her previous history, she was once again suffering from relationships with men that led to rejection and fear of being alone. She had an adult son with whom she felt very close.

Her caretaker personality repeatedly set her up for rejection. She was exploited principally (both financially and emotionally) by her mother, but also by siblings, friends, and lovers. She was always picking losers and always wound up being disappointed, rejected, angry and depressed. I was probably her sole source of emotional support. In spite of the insight I provided, she repeatedly fell into romantic and family relationships that were never going to work. She was a very hard worker and, in spite of a lack of family support, she had attained an associate's degree and was successful at her job. Unfortunately, in the past decade, her physical health has seriously compromised her ability to work and has led to a loss of employment.

In the very recent past, she was once again exploited financially by a sibling. She also had difficulty adjusting to the death of the mother. She no longer could nourish fantasies that her mother would eventually love her instead of exploiting her. She entered into an affair with one gentleman on three separate occasions. He was unfaithful to her the whole time. Of course, she was very angry and became distressed at the loss of what she believed was a loving relationship.

I am describing this person to point out how persistently someone can strive to get what is needed emotionally from others who are incapable of giving it to her or him. For this patient, doing so was obviously an attempt to try again to get the emotional support she had not gotten in childhood and adulthood up to the present time. These repeated attempts never work, because many choose the same kind of people who disappointed them in the past. My patient is an excellent caretaker, and caretakees are always lying in wait to exploit that quality for their benefit without reciprocating with the caretaker.

Although this patient generally has a good relationship with the adult son, he occasionally tried to take advantage of her. For example, he needed to purchase a means of transportation and asked for a loan, which she readily gave him. However, an accident caused a total loss. Her insurance company paid him for the loss, but several months later he still had not repaid his mother. I asked her to bring him in to the next session and he complied. He repaid her. This showed me how difficult it was for her to stand up for herself instead of allowing herself to be exploited because she needed his love.

One last note in this regard. She recently met another man whom she described as the nicest guy she ever met. I was quite happy for her. I did not see her for several months, and when she returned she stated, "You know I am not quite sure of this relationship. It may not be exciting." I replied, "You mean there is not as much excitement as there is when you embark on a journey with a loser that you are going to convince to love you?" She laughed, knowing exactly what I meant.

This scenario demonstrates out how persistent we can be to undo past emotional failure. I would also emphasize the excitement there is in thinking, "I will make it work this time and finally come to believe I am lovable and I can feel good about myself." As previously stated, I believe caretakers marry caretakees. The problem is, in many marriages, the discrepancy between the empathy of the caretaker and the caretakee is too great and makes adjustments too difficult and failure too frequent.

Here is another example of this patient's ongoing conflict about separation from her family is.

She described a recent episode of behavior toward her brother, younger than she and unmarried, telling her that he was thinking of buying a parcel of land in a rural area that would comprise a significant amount of acreage. Without any request for financial help on his part, she rushed in to offer money. She was not in any way capable of taking on that obligation. In any event, he told her he decided against making an offer. She was devastated that he had changed his mind. When relating the example to me in the session, she was still distraught and crying. She openly admitted she thought he should have his dream fulfilled by her. I explained how the episode was characteristic of her need to go out of her way to meet the needs of her parents and siblings no matter how unreasonable it was. Of course, this was the only way she felt she had a chance to get the love of her family members. This had been a lifelong pattern. She stated, "I knew when I made the offer that I was wrong, but I couldn't stop myself. Even though I knew what position you would take."

This demonstrates the tremendous effort we make to overcome the less than adequate love received in our childhood. It is terribly difficult to come to terms with the emotional pain of childhood. We hate to give up the dream of being loved by people who cannot give it, and we unfortunately keep trying to get it from the same family or from other people who are going to frustrate us in the same way.

Case Study 8

A man, in his 30s and never married, came for help with symptoms that seemed related to elements of depression and anxiety over the previous year. About a decade before, he had sought help from a therapist on three different occasions for only several visits at a time. He described himself as a "worrier since childhood." Both parents suffered with depression, and it appeared that a younger male sibling was having difficulty getting motivated to find a stable career. The patient remembered being worried in his childhood about the marital strife in his parents, as well as money issues.

The patient was working steadily when we started treatment. His visits were infrequent but fruitful. He initially refused medication, but then tried several only to stop because of side effects. This anxiety about side effects often indicates a perfectionist personality that is afraid of anything he can't absolutely control. However, the patient did finally accept a particular antidepressant, which he took during the several years of treatment with me.

At the time of our first meeting, he complained of having difficulty relating emotionally to a woman who repeatedly berated him for seemingly no reason. They had been dating for two years, and he had moved in with her six months previously. She was at least a decade older than he. In an effort to improve their relationship, he asked permission to bring her in. My patient later reported that he gained insight in our first meeting with his girlfriend, but she didn't believe she had gained anything. In a second meeting, I tried to point out to her how some aspect of her behavior was only making matters worse. She immediately became furious and stormed out of the room.

As I stated previously, this patient came to see me periodically at time intervals decided by him. I was comfortable with that arrangement. It wasn't until later in the course of our therapy that I realized he was somewhat cautious about the cost involved with treatment.

On his next visit, he spoke of separating from the girlfriend and finding another. This woman was also older, although not quite as much as the previous girlfriend. The relationship was not as traumatic as the first one, but it also was not entirely satisfactory. In thinking about his attractions to older women, I believed he was a careta-kee looking for a caretaker mother. However, his descriptions of his interactions with them showed him to be much more in a caretaker role than a caretakee role. I therefore changed my mind about his personality characteristics and told him that I was wrong about my initial impressions.

During the next visit he stated, "I told my mother that you believe I am a caretaker, and she said, 'Oh, I have always known this since you were a little boy.'" What the mother didn't add was how much she benefited emotionally from his caretaking. I believe the child born a caretaker is often used psychologically by a needy parent or parents, siblings, or by friends.

In regard to my patient's relationships, I would suggest he was attracted to older women. He was replaying the role he played as a child, i.e., using caretaker qualities to get the mother to reciprocate with emotional support. He was searching to feel good about himself and was not getting enough in return. The mother was taking more than she was giving.

I have come to believe that this discrepancy in the mother's ability to give when the child is giving his best produces a great deal of anger, much of which often needs to be repressed. He was replaying that same role with the women he chose as partners with the same result. When he first came to see me, I believe that repressed anger was triggering the neurotransmitters to produce symptoms of anxiety and depression.

On his most recent and perhaps his last visit, he was feeling much improved. He had just broken up with a girlfriend who was only slightly older than he. When I asked why, he stated, "She was unbelievably needy." He stated that it was our last visit. He felt well and at this point had no need for psychotherapy. His insurance had changed and he believed the co-pay was too expensive. This was in keeping with his close attention to expenses and budgeting and his most recent purchase of a house, in which he planned to live and also rent out an apartment. He would ask the primary physician to oversee his meds.

I must point out that when he first came to see me, he had focused mainly on his relationship to women. However, there was additionally some significant work stress which resolved later. This too was adding to his anger, which brought on his symptomology. ▪

This patient was in her 70s when she was referred to me. She had been seeing another psychiatrist that left his practice. I was told by the family that he had diagnosed her as having an addiction to tranquilizers. Her husband, who was a physician, referred her to me. They had a couple of adult children who were married and no longer living at home.

As treatment progressed, I never saw any abuse of tranquilizers. What I realized was that the only time she used tranquilizers was when she was stressed by her husband, and even then she never abused them. The stress was relatively ongoing. He was unbelievably needy. He exemplified the caretakee, and this had been going on since the beginning of their relationship and marriage. Also the stress was much greater around any holiday when a family would normally expect to be together, having guests and enjoying themselves. The husband always found a way to make this time unpleasant and induce unreasonable stress in the patient. He was always highly critical and lacked any sympathy for her. This is typical of the caretakee. It goes like this: don't let the caretaker know how valuable she is to you; instead convince her that she is loaded with deficiencies in her personality that make her believe she is anything but worthwhile. Always cut her down so that she won't feel worthwhile and confident in herself. The husband always found a way to keep her at home. He saw no reason for her to go on a vacation or to enjoy traveling, especially to see different museums – her favorite activity.

During my treatment of her, the husband required surgery that disabled him. Of course, she was there for him and he behaved much better. She was optimistic regarding the improvement. He exhibited a cooperative and pleasant attitude, which made her feel better. I warned her that it wouldn't last and that he would revert to negative behavior of criticizing her as soon as he was able to return to normal health. Of course, he did exactly as I predicted. The old pattern returned and continued to negatively affect my patient.

On one occasion, the patient pointedly asked me what she could do to change things. I mentioned she could consider separation or even divorce. One time, quite by accident, I encountered her husband in the hospital where we both worked and he inquired, "How is my wife doing?" I replied she could be doing much better if he treated her better. He never asked again.

When her husband suddenly died, the patient was sad but handled it well. During her next therapy session, she asked if I would direct her in how to discontinue her psychotropic medication. I set up a plan. I knew she wouldn't have any trouble, and on her next visit she informed me that she had discontinued the medications. She believed she was handling any grief she had very well. We both felt she didn't need to schedule another appointment unless she had a return of symptoms.

One day as I was waiting on an elevator in the hospital garage building, the door opened and she was there with her brother. She was very happy to see me and gave me a big hug. She then related to me all the wonderful places she had visited around the world, especially the museums. She was enjoying life as never before.

Once again this is an example of people making other people sick. It is an example of a caretaker being ground down from struggling with a very, very needy caretakee and becoming more and more angry and then becoming anxious and depressed. ▓

Case Study 10

A married man, in his late 20s with a wife and children, consulted me many years ago. I can't give a lengthy history, but I believe the study shows how much a caretaker can fall ill due to circumstances rather than conflict with others.

He was happily married and there were no conflicts with his or his wife's families. He presented to me with the chief complaint of being progressively more depressed. He was treated with psychotherapy and medication and had at least one hospitalization. There was no improvement and he was getting steadily worse.

I soon realized his trouble lay with his work life. He had been an excellent worker who was the intermediary between management and the labor union. He was respected by both management and the labor union. Because of his success, management promoted and transferred him to a different location. He was successful at his new job and consequently was transferred back to the parent company and promoted once again. His depression started after his last promotion and return to the parent company. He was working in a cubicle with little social contact and, as he described it, "just shuffling papers." In his previous job, he commingled with the workers in the plant, inquiring about their concerns. He experienced a great deal of pleasure in those relationships with workers and managers.

In my opinion, he couldn't have had a better job for his caretaker personality and emotional needs. He was very strongly attached to his work. As with all attachments large or small, when they are taken away from us, we suffer anger, and the longer it goes on, the more we are unable to adjust to the change. We can become depressed, anxious, psychosomatic, etc.

When I realized how much he was attached to his old job, I had a meeting with him and his wife and explained my understanding of why he was depressed. The wife concurred with my diagnosis and began a search for another job for her husband. She found one for him in a different part of the country and they moved.

He began to improve immediately. The wife sent me Christmas cards for several years informing me that he was asymptomatic and they were quite happy with his new job.

I presented this case to emphasize how one can be so deeply attached to something and not be consciously aware of it. If he had realized his attachment to working in relationship with others, the patient might have been more careful about accepting a promotion that was going to take away this strong attachment and cause him to become depressed. In general, we do not realize how many attachments we have and how they support our lives emotionally. I believe the loss of any attachment that makes us feel better about ourselves causes anger. The anger is added to our reservoir of anger that is largely unconscious and has been made better or worse by the positive attachments we have had since birth. You can project the anger outward and hurt others or inward and get depressed. This patient's dramatic change for the better shows the power of attachment and the emotional pain it can cause if lost. ▪

Case Study 11

A woman came to see me years ago because she was depressed. Significant in the history she related was that she had a great friendship with a good girlfriend. It was a healthy relationship in which both were mature and gave freely emotionally. Unfortunately, the other woman's mother became very ill and required the friend to devote a considerable amount of time to her care.

My patient realized that her friend was a good caretaker and would, of course, take excellent care of her mother. The patient and I worked in psychotherapy for many months along with medication. After some months, she improved and was convinced that I had made her well. In reality, the girlfriend's mother died and, in due time, she was able to resume the relationship with her friend and became free of the depression. I thanked her for the compliment, but I explained that the return of the friendship cured her.

One could ask, "so what is the big deal? Why did you believe it was necessary to add this very short example to cases?" The only answer I have to that question is the effect it had on me as a young psychiatrist early in my private practice. I realized how painful it was to lose such a valuable attachment to another human being and how healing it can be to get it back.

Since then and particularly in the recent past, I have become convinced of the importance of anger resulting from the losses of our attachments of all kinds. Retrospectively in this particular example, the anger my patient experienced was turned inward on herself and she became depressed.

Definitions

Anger: A feeling of displeasure resulting from injury, mistreatment, opposition, etc., and usually showing itself as a desire to fight back at the supposed cause of this feeling.

Aggression: In psychiatry, forceful attacking behavior, either constructively self-assertive and self-protective or destructively hostile to others or oneself.

Cathexis: The concentration of psychic energy on some particular person, thing, idea or aspect of the self.

Consciousness: The state of being conscious; awareness of one's own feelings, what is happening around one, etc. The totality of one's thoughts, feelings and impressions; the conscious mind.

Hypothesis: An unproved theory, proposition, or supposition tentatively accepted to explain certain facts, as in a working hypothesis to provide a basis for further investigation, argument, etc.

Instinct: An inborn tendency to behave in a way characteristic of a species; a natural, unlearned, predictable response to stimuli. (Sucking is an instinct in mammals.)

Repress: To force ideas, impulses, etc. that are painful to the conscious mind into the unconscious. To prevent such ideas or impulses from reaching the level of consciousness.

References

Aggression. (2014). In Webster's *New World College Dictionary* (5th ed.). (2014). Boston, MA: Houghton Mifflin Harcourt Publishing Company.

Anger. (2014). In Webster's *New World College Dictionary* (5th ed.). Boston, MA: Houghton Mifflin Harcourt Publishing Company.

Auchincloss, E. L., & Glick, R. A. (1996). The psychoanalytic model of the mind. In R. Michels (Ed.), *Textbook of Psychoanalysis*. New York, NY: Lippincott-Raven, pp. 1–29.

Birth trauma. (2012). In G. O. Gabbard, B. E. Litowitz, & P. Williams (Eds.), *Textbook of Psychoanalysis* (2nd ed.). Arlington, VA: American Psychiatric Publishing, p. 569.

Bond. (2014). In Webster's *New World College Dictionary* (5th ed.). Boston, MA: Houghton Mifflin Harcourt Publishing Company, p. 168.

Bowlby, J. (1969–1980). *Attachment and loss* (Vols. 1–3). New York, NY: Basic Books.

Bowlby, J. (1988). *A secure base: Clinical applications of attachment theory.* London, England: Routledge.

Brown, S. A., Kunz, D., Dumas, A., Westermark, P. O.,...Kramer, A. (2008). Molecular insights into human behavior. *Proceedings of the National Academy of Sciences of the United States of America, 105(5),* 1602–7.

Congreve, W. (1697). *The Mourning Bride,* as spoken by Perez, Act 3, Scene 2.

Diamond, J. (2006). *Collapse: How societies choose to fail or succeed,* (Rev. ed.). New York, NY: Penguin.

Ellenberger, H. (1970). *The discovery of the unconscious: The history and evolution of dynamic psychiatry.* New York, NY: Basic Books.

Empathy. (2001). In Webster's *New World College Dictionary* (4th ed.). Foster City, CA: IDG Books Worldwide, Inc.

Heinlein, R. A. (2016, December 20). As quoted in *Forbes Magazine* (p. 112).

Jones, E. (1953–1957). *The life and work of Sigmund Freud* (Vols. 1–3). New York, NY: Basic Books, Inc.

Klein, M. (2002). Love, guilt, and reparation: And other works 1921–1945. New York, NY: Simon & Schuster.

Lorenz, K. (1963). *On aggression.* Translated by Marjorie Kerr Wilson. New York, NY: Harcourt, Brace, and World, Inc.

Lumsden, C. J., & Wilson, E. O. (1983). *Promethean fire: Reflections of the origin of mind.* Cambridge, MA: Harvard University Press.

Roth, M. (2006, January 30). Researchers say toddlers are most violent. *Pittsburgh Post Gazette.*

Schweitzer, A., & Joy, C. R. (1947). *Albert Schweitzer: An anthology.* New York, NY: Harper and Brothers, p. 73.

Strachey, J., & Freud, F. (Eds.). (1961). *The standard edition of the complete psychological works of Sigmund Freud* (vols 1–24). London, England: The Hogarth Press.

Williams, P. (2012). Object relations. In G. O. Gabbard, B. E. Litowitz, & P. Williams (Eds.), *Textbook of Psychoanalysis* (2nd ed.). Arlington, VA: American Psychiatric Publishing, p. 171–184.

Wilson, E. O. (2012). *The social conquest of earth.* New York, NY: Liveright Publishing Corporation.

Wilson, E. O., & Dennett, D. C. (201). Evolutionary philosophy. In A. Bly (ed.), *Science is culture: Conversations at the new intersection of science and society.* New York, NY: Harper Collins Publishing, pp. 1–23.

About the Author

Lester Bolanovich, M.D., has been a psychiatrist in Pittsburgh, Pennsylvania, where he has treated patients with a variety of mental health issues for the past 60 years. After graduating from the University of Pittsburgh School of Medicine in 1951, he served a 12-month general rotating internship at St. Francis General Hospital in Pittsburgh. The hospital had approximately three hundred beds devoted primarily to psychiatric patients. Following his internship, he spent two years in a psychiatric residency program there. His third year of psychiatric residency began in July 1954, at the Western Psychiatric Institute and Clinic in Pittsburgh, but was interrupted by a two-year stint in the U.S. Navy (1954–1956). During that time, he was assigned to the Naval Hospital at Camp LeJeune in Jacksonville, North Carolina, treating both military personnel and their families.

After his Navy service, Dr. Bolanovich returned to his psychiatric residency at the Western Psychiatric Institute and Clinic. Upon completing his residency in 1957, he started a general psychiatric practice seeing both office and hospitalized patients. Within several years, he applied for and was admitted as a candidate to the University of Pittsburgh Psychoanalytic Institute Training Program. He graduated in 1969 and was certified by the American Psychoanalytic Association in 1973. During these years, he was active in supervising psychiatric residents in both hospitals where he trained. He also had the pleasure of teaching some courses at the Pittsburgh Psychoanalytic Institute. In 2017, he was certified by the American Board of Psychoanalysis. He presently is continuing his office practice and enjoying it.